MW00937023

Kerianne Mellott

Learn to Go Live: Conquer Your Fears,
Reach Through the Lens and Pick Up
Money on the Table

Copyright © by KERIANNE MELLOTT

LEARN TO GO LIVE: CONQUER YOUR FEARS, REACH
THROUGH THE LENS & PICK UP MONEY ON THE
TABLE

**Cover art by Anabella Feaugas**

Copyright © 2019 by Kerianne Mellott

# Acknowledgements

Special thanks to everyone who helped make this book a reality. I feel so blessed to have an amazing support system around me. You all truly help push me to go after my dreams and goals.

Thank you to everyone in the Paparazzi Accessories family. You are my fabulously fancy five dollar jewelry bling bosses! To all the Support Staff, Independent Consultants, and the Elite team leaders who have allowed me to help them on this journey in some way, shape or form. You are all beautiful souls, on the inside and out.

To Lissy Botman for finding me one day on a women's entrepreneurs Facebook group and seeing the potential of a great partnership. Without the support, encouragement, hilarious GIF conversations at 2am on Messenger and consistent faith in me and my leadership skills this book wouldn't be a thing, and my business wouldn't be where it is today. I am SO grateful to you for all your hard work.

To Dr. Ron Koperski, my Public Relations

professor in college, who saw a young, bright, determined, divorced single mom, and knew she was capable of making a difference in the world before she ever got started. Thank you for believing in me and for helping open the door to my new world in Los Angeles.

To James Kinney for constantly challenging me to uplevel, and for helping me hold the highest version of myself in clear sight at all times. You inspire me daily with who you are and how you move in this world. Thank you for your endless love and support.

And to my son, Austin James, who I'm going to thank in ALL of my books. Thank you for your patience, your intuition, your understanding and your encouragement. You're the very reason I find strength, fortitude and tenacity to do what I do and serve so many people so you know what it'll look like when it's your turn. You are incredible and I love you so much.

# Table of Contents

*A Note from the Author:*

*Stuff changes in technology and business all the time, but Social Media changes at warp speed. Some things in this book might not work in the future. They might have features or products that have been taken away, improved upon, or enhanced. Strategies I give you today may not work once everyone gets ahold of them. It's all constantly evolving and adapting. One of the many reasons why this is my first book after working in this industry for over 14 years is because it's impossible to write something that doesn't become outdated the minute it goes to press. With that said, this information is too important to keep to myself! Please enjoy the content with an understanding that some stuff may change.*

*Rules at companies outside of Facebook, Instagram, etc change, too. Things that are cool to do today as I write this book may not be cool to do in the future. It might get better. It might get worse. Always be sure you're compliant with your company's policies and procedures for selling online.*

*All I know is that RIGHT NOW, my friend, here's what's working. So congrats on getting your hands on this timely knowledge. The window has just opened - it's time to step into your digital spotlight!*

# Introduction

Hello! My name is Kerianne Mellott and I'm a Marketing Coach and Social Media Expert. I've been using social media marketing for business for over 14 years now so I'll proudly take the title of "social media dinosaur!" It's impossible to know everything in such a fast-paced and ever-changing industry such as social media. However, I do know a lot more than most people who are just picking this up in recent years or months. I feel compelled to (finally) share my knowledge in a book! This book shares with you the most powerful tool I've come across in over a decade - especially if you're a small business owner or entrepreneur. We're, of course, talking about using live video on social media.

Btw, I'm also not afraid of embracing age and recognizing I'm "old" as my teenage son calls me when he's showing me the latest Snapchat feature. You might be feeling intimidated by all these young whippersnappers because they get this stuff pretty dang quick, but that's ok! You're still perfectly capable of learning new things, mastering new skills and crushing it in business. We'll also address FEAR and how what other people might think of you affects your potential success - no matter how old you are.

Speaking of age, later on we'll address any hangups you might have about what you look like on camera. We can't have our high-school bodies back, but I have plenty of experience (plus tips and tricks) from living and working in Los Angeles, CA and overcoming my "not-so-perfect" flaws.

I'm here to help make you look and FEEL like a million bucks - just where you are right now. It's totally possible.

Speaking of the City of Angels, I never thought I'd end up living in the 2nd largest city in the US for such a long time. I'm originally from Illinois and spent my later years as a teenager living on a farm in a super small town of about 1,000 people. It was there, however, where I was given the opportunity

to start discovering what confidence looks like.

For over a decade, I worked in LA, and it was

taking the huge leap of faith in relocating there to

further my career that ultimately led me to writing

this book for you.  Besides the perfect weather

year-round, the opportunities to grow in your life

and business there are endless.  My experiences

include working for AT&T, Paul Mitchell the

School, and eHarmony, where I was the Director of

Social Media.  As a former corporate executive

working for a major brand, I intend to share my

experiences with you to help bring you new insight

about major concepts and theories of what's

working and what's not.  Social Media has leveled

the playing field and whether you're a

one-man/one-woman show, or heading up a major

corporation, everyone needs to be leveraging social

media platforms.  It's no longer just a trend.

Part of the learning process for you will be

reflecting back throughout your life to see how all

of your experiences shaped you - and you'll realize

what makes YOU truly unique and special.  You'll

also learn how to bring this out on camera.

I'm an early adopter of all techy things and social

media stuff and was always thrilled when my team

at Facebook or Twitter or Google would tell me

about a new product they'd created that we could

use for our campaigns.  (Pro tip: Figuring things out

BEFORE everyone else gives you a leg up on your competition - ESPECIALLY in social media. #winning)

One day several years ago, my favorite Twitter Account Executive for eHarmony flew down from San Francisco to the office for a meeting. He then took my team and me out to dinner that night. After a productive day of work and a fantastic meal at a steakhouse right on the Pacific Ocean, he took out his phone at the table and said, "Kerianne...I have to show you something."

He started pressing a few buttons. I saw his camera start working and then he started talking to his screen.

"Hi, guys!" he said, excitedly.

His camera was open and his face was on the screen - he had started a live broadcast on Periscope (Twitter's live streaming solution).  Immediately people at Twitter Headquarters were jumping on and began to leave their comments.

He turned the phone screen towards me and said, "Guys, meet Kerianne from eHarmony!"

I was nervous and flabbergasted...but totally in awe. There was immediate response - in real-time! What kind of voodoo magic was this?!

We carried on a brief conversation about what he was showing me, and he showed them the beautiful steakhouse we were at, as we got up and walked outside to wait for our cars in Valet. They were chatting up a storm with us and leaving comments - in REAL TIME!

As hearts floated up the screen in admiration and approval of what was happening right then and there, it was in that moment I realized how amazing this new tool was going to be.  I mean....how cool was that?! It was like they were with us.

It was my job to figure out how to make this work for business.

I had to learn how to conquer MY fears of getting

on camera, learn how to create an effective live

broadcast and ultimately "move the needle" (or in

biz terms...make money) from it.

We had a 220% return on our investment during our

first big live streaming campaign at eHarmony.  Not

only did we make the company money, but there's a

good chance some lives were changed in a big way

after people saw our campaign and decided to sign

up for a subscription to find their "person" and fall

in love.  INCREDIBLE results!

We also used Facebook Live to accomplish other

important goals such as offering customer service

(most brands are scared of being so exposed due to

possible angry customers - I say embrace it),

promotions, Q&A, PR announcements,

behind-the-scenes at the office, employee

spotlights, brand awareness campaigns, contests,

Facebook Live broadcasts where the CEO makes

cocktails at the office on a Friday afternoon (he

always made a point to connect with his employees

and build relationships), and more.

I also started using live streaming myself and built a

following and engaged audience who I'd connect

with often.  I remember streaming Live at the office

during the day, then coming home after a long day

and crashing on my bed, only to start my own

personal broadcasts where I had a blast re-capping

the day, talking with friends, sharing funny stories

and more.  It's an amazing tool.

After I left corporate America and returned to being
a full-time Marketing Coach in 2017, I turned to the
most powerful tool I'd found in my career to build
up my personal brand - Facebook Live.  To be able
to connect with tens of thousands of REAL
PEOPLE in a short period of time, in one easy
strategy, is a priceless gift.  To be able to build
those precious relationships, add value to their lives
and then monetize your efforts is simply
tremendous.  You MUST realize the gold that's
been given to us and take full advantage of it!

My goal for you in this book is to help give you the
confidence and education on how you can build a

successful live streaming strategy, too. If you apply

everything you've learned and keep at it, you'll be

amazed at the growth of your business.

# Chapter One:  Why You HAVE to Learn This

**Why should you go Live?**

**The first  obvious and most significant answer if you're in business is to make money**.

You most certainly will learn how to reach through the lens and pick up money on the table.  That being said, you can go Live for a NUMEROUS amount of reasons.  And if you pick up what I'm putting down in this book, you'll see how different approaches all work together to contribute to your bottom line.

Now, I hope this next part doesn't come as a shock

to you, but every single financial gain or transaction

you make comes from a human being. A

relationship. Even if you're walking down the

street and find a $20 bill on the ground, a HUMAN

dropped it. Even if a robot helps you make a

purchase through an automated process, humans

probably built it and are there watching.

The cool part about social media is that HUMANS

log on to their profiles multiple times every day.

They also have MONEY! Therefore, you're in the

perfect place to learn this skill of going Live to get

in front of the right ones who want what you have

and will pay you for it. I like getting to the money

without begging, struggling or feeling overwhelmed. Learning how to go Live accomplishes this goal so you can actually feel great about getting paid, baby. If I told you all you had to be was yourself, talk about and/or show what you have to offer and then you'd make money, is that cool with you? Yeah, I thought so.

**Another reason you have to do this is to be an example to others**.

Whether that means you have a team that looks up to you, or have goals to build a large team in business, then you have a responsibility to be an example to them. A leader is all about "do what I DO" not "do what I SAY." Once you rip the bandaid off and start mastering your live streaming

skillz, you're gonna start to see others do the same

thing. If you find a system that works, work it! But

definitely learn how to do this. Do this for yourself

- and for them.

**Third, social media is a big playground. Stake**

**your territory.**

In the Introduction I said that being an early adopter

is amazing when it comes to these social media

platforms. Why? Because there's less competition

at the beginning of something. Simple as that. If

not that many people are doing it, then you don't

have to compete for people's attention as much.

Boom! Your Live video on Facebook, for example,

will catch more people's attention than someone's (boring) article they may have just posted. We'd much rather watch you!

We live in such a cool time in history to be in business. We're smack dab in the middle of The Information Age. Technology is your best friend. Use it! Leverage it! Put your flag in the digital ground and claim it as yours. It's a land grab right now.

The generation behind you didn't have this opportunity to sit at their house, grab their phone, click on an "app" and make money from a room in their house, did they? Nope! They ALL had to get up and leave their house to go get that paper. Just stop and think about what a blessing technology and social media is in your business for a minute. Don't take it for granted.

That being said, you have been given a small window of time to figure this out. You know by now that all of this social media stuff and technology moves fast, right? It's constantly evolving, changing, adding, re-arranging, removing things that don't catch on or work, building new things that can help you CRUSH IT, etc. At some point, even this book will be outdated. Everyone will know how to do this (maybe from watching YOU after you've mastered this!), and soon it'll be more competitive and harder to make money. For the simple fact alone that you've caught this at the early part of it becoming a "thing" means you need

to jump on this NOW. When you make the

decision to really do this, come up with a strong

personal brand and a strategy of how you're going

to "perform" for your audiences whenever you go

Live, you can win. Like, big time.

**Lastly, you HAVE to add this amazing tool to**

**your Marketing toolbox because as we speak,**

**Facebook's big priority is video.**

Video, video, video. And more specifically, LIVE

video.

It's no question that Facebook is the big 800-lb.

gorilla in this space, leading the way with Live

video.  They simply have the most users.

Throughout the book I may refer mostly to

Facebook but the strategies and concepts will pretty

much apply to any social media platform where

you're given a digital stage to perform on.


Let me tell you why Live video is so important

today.


Have you heard of the Facebook algorithm?

Essentially, an algorithm is defined as the

following:


**al·go·rithm**

[ˈalgəˌriT͟Həm]

NOUN

1. a process or set of rules to be followed in calculations or other problem-solving operations, especially by a computer.

2. "a basic algorithm for division"

For Facebook, the problem it's trying to solve is how they can organize your Newsfeed in a way that makes sure you're happy with what you're seeing, the Advertisers are happy that their Ads are being served up to you, and that meaningful connections are being made by all.

I won't go into full detail here about how it works (they also don't share the very specific calculations publicly...just highlights and what they're trying to accomplish with a new change to their formula) but

I can tell you that as much angst or bad rap that the Facebook algorithm gets ("Why is no one seeing my posts??? Ugh...stupid algorithm...smh") that you should be GLAD for the formula.

Essentially, there are so many things posted to Facebook all day long (ie - pics of your friend's kids, viral videos, funny memes, posts about a friend checking into the gym, pictures of someone's new inventory they just got, etc) that if someone didn't organize them and show you just a portion of it all instead of EVERY.SINGLE.POST. you'd go mad. Like, it'd be impossible to see EVERY POST, from EVERY friend or Page or Group that you follow, EVERY DAY. RIGHT?!

Ohmygoodness I'm overwhelmed and my thumb

hurts just thinking about what that'd look like and how I'd find the time to scroll through and look at every single thing. Impossible. And if you have more than 100 friends, belong to at least 5 groups and have "Liked" at least 25 Pages, imagine how much content this would be from everybody in just one day! It's literally a firehose of posts.

Thank GOODNESS someone (aka Facebook's computers) organize it for us, based on what it thinks we want to see the most. The coolest part is that it's unique to YOU.

This special formula learns about you. It doesn't just make its own decisions for you about what to show you every time you hop on your phone or

computer to start scrolling. No sir, no ma'am. It watches who you interact with, how often you interact with them and to what level. Are you just scrolling through? Are you "liking" stuff? Or are you "loving" stuff? The algorithm knows the difference. Are you leaving comments? Are you going to other people's profiles or clicking through to certain groups? Or are you just staying put in the Newsfeed each time you log on? The algorithm knows what you like to do and who you like to interact with. It's going to keep you happy with what you continue to show it how you behave on there, not start throwing you posts from someone you've never really talked to before. Doesn't it make sense that if you're liking something for them to keep giving you more of that? It's as if you always go to your favorite restaurant and order the

same thing all the time because you love it.

Eventually the waitress knows you by name and

brings you your order of a cheeseburger and fries

(no pickle, tomatoes on the side) without you even

asking for it. You smile all big and keep repeating

the process. You'd be totally thrown off if Miss

Diner Girl one day brought you a plate of liver and

onions, right? Girl, bye. You didn't ask for that!


Same thing with the algorithm. It's all math and

science. A computer program just working on

keeping you happy. :)


So why am I bringing up the Facebook algorithm in

a book at about learning to go Live? Because I said

that right now Facebook is favoring video, and

more specifically Live videos.  Which MEANS,

that if you all of a sudden find yourself some extra

time to post on Facebook and you think "Hmm...I

could just make a post about how these new

products just got added to my website..." or

"Hmm....I could go Live and tell people who I am,

what I sell and even show them some of my

products that I have on-hand..." Facebook will

reward you by choosing to go Live instead of just a

post because the algorithm FAVORS Facebook

Live video posts.  This means they'll show your

Facebook Live video to more people in the

Newsfeed than your post with words or pictures.

Currently, that number is six TIMES more than any

other type of post!

And the name of the game is to capture people's

ATTENTION so they can see what ya got. You

want as many eyeballs as possible on your stuff,

right?!

So, if you're scared or don't have a solid strategy of

what to do when you get on camera (hint: having an

amazing "show" is part of the success formula

here), now is the time to conquer your fears and

create an amazing gameplan. Both Facebook and I

are behind ya, cheering you on!

So can I get you to agree that it's time to appreciate

the Facebook algorithm for all of its hard work on

our behalf and know that it's gonna show you off to

more people when you go Live? Yes? Ok.

Awesome.

**Ok, So Now You Agree That You Have to Do This….But Here's Why Going Live on Social Media Matters RIGHT NOW**

Let's go for a second back to 2003 when I was getting my Bachelor's Degree in Advertising and Marketing.  Facebook was meant for only for us college kids.  MySpace was dominating.  How we know social media today was not even a thing.

I was learning about all the ways to best promote a product or service.  We learned about TV commercials, radio ads, magazine ads, billboards, etc. These places to advertise are known as Traditional Media. Cool. These were the days of TGIF where families (including my own) would gather around the TV every Friday night and watch sitcom after sitcom. RELIGIOUSLY! We couldn't wait for those shows to come on. And do you remember what we saw all throughout those shows? Commercials.

You don't need a degree in Advertising to know that today only a super teeny tiny percentage of families still have this tradition of TV dinners and quality bonding time around the 'tube. And while billboards, radio programming, newspapers and magazine are still here, gone are the days of focused attention on just these main media outlets. Gone are the days from everyone's eyeballs on one TV

screen, watching one show, and catching all the

commercials throughout the 30-minutes.


So, where is everyone's eyeballs today instead?

You know it - tiny, hand-held screens! They're on

phones, tablets, PS4 devices and more. Almost

everyone has a smartphone...and what's on the

smartphone? APPS! Netflix, Hulu, Amazon,

YouTube...and these are just video content sources.

Then we look at social media apps and based on

data, over 1 BILLION people are spending time on

Facebook...and a large percentage log in multiple

times a day!  Some people have no idea where the

TV remote is, but their phone is typically

ALWAYS near their body.

So...yes, the world in Advertising has changed
drastically. Technology and the fact that consumers
can purchase more things online than ever before
has literally seen major brands file for bankruptcy.
RIP....Toys 'R Us, Blockbuster Video, and Claire's,
just to name a few. (As sad as this is, I see this now
as a huge opportunity if you know how to make
social media work for you in biz.)

So if Advertisers aren't happy with the staggering
decline of viewer's eyeballs no longer gathered
around the family TV every Friday night to catch
their million dollar :30 commercials, what do you
think they need to do?

Find where the eyeballs went.

And you and I both already know where they are -

on places like Facebook, Instagram and YouTube!

This is where you come in.

In order to keep people's attention on places like

Facebook, they need good content for their users to

watch. This is one of the reasons why they've

launched things on their new video platform of

shows, Facebook Watch.

But BEST BELIEVE - they want YOU to create

good content, too.

For example, on Instagram (an app that is owned by Facebook) you have what are called "Stories." They live on Facebook, too, and you're seeing them at the top of your Newsfeeds now. These are short clips of pics or videos you can share that expire every 24 hours. Guess what's sandwiched in between every few stories? A Sponsored Ad - from an Advertiser. They've paid money to be there, in front of your eyeballs. Mixed in among the content you're watching already from your friends and people/brands you follow. Most of these Ads ask you to "swipe up" and take action to go to their website, learn more, make a purchase, etc.

But, imagine if none of the users posted any stories.

The advertisers would say, "Hey! There's nobody here. We're not going to pay for that….no one will see our Ad.  We need eyeballs!"

So the social media platforms and the Advertisers need you as a user to post content.  We'd all leave if none of our friends posted and it was just a Newsfeed of Ads, right?  See how that works?

Learning how to go Live for your business on your special Facebook Page creates extra good content for the Facebook community.  It brings value (more about "The Top 3 Categories of Value" you need to create later) and makes the users, Advertisers and Facebook happy.  Looking like a high-quality production or "show" when you go Live is key here, too. But first things first. We'll get there.

Speaking of big brands and Advertisers, do you
realize that YOU could create an Advertising
campaign and have your business featured in one of
those Sponsored Ads you see on Facebook or
Instagram? That's right. Right alongside the big
brands like Nike, Coca Cola and more. Social
Media companies have leveled the playing field and
they've made a dream come true for the small
business owner or entrepreneur - the ability to
advertise to the same people the big brands are
trying to speak to as well. Once you know the inner
workings of running a social media Ad campaign,
your mind will be blown. (And I'm not talking
about just boosting a post. It's more complex than

that.) And yes, it costs money, but you don't need millions of dollars to make a big impact for your business. You need good content, and you can even turn a FB Live video into a paid Ad campaign on your Page. Pretty cool, right?

Speaking of millions of dollars, I've been privileged to have worked with major brands who DO spend millions of dollars on Advertising. I've been on set of these nationwide TV commercials and seen the hard work that goes into making a :15 or :30 spot. But I've also been on set myself, in front of the camera, presenting content on video to our social media audiences. It's a different vibe. The goals might be the same but the way it's produced and delivered are very different.

In my opinion, anytime a brand or business can be more relatable - more HUMAN - the better. After all, transactions of money being exchanged happen between people. We like to feel connected with others. This is the secret sauce of social media platforms for business owners or entrepreneurs. You get the ability to run a business but by appearing human and real and authentic and caring about your audience, you make money by earning their trust and them becoming a customer of yours.

As we move throughout this book, you'll learn specifically how to do this. I'm excited, are you?! Let's keep going.

# Chapter Two: Stepping Into Your Digital Spotlight

Before we dig into the nitty gritty of how to actually go Live on social media, we need to cover the biggest hurdle of it all.  FEAR.

Even if you've ripped off the band-aid and have done some Live broadcasts already, I'm willing to bet you're still not playing at a level that you're capable of...am I right? Is there more you could be doing? Of course there is.  As my teenage son says, "You gotta play FULL SEND, Mom!" I'm not sure what "full send" means, or where he got that from, but I feel the energy when he says it to me and

reminds me I could be doing even more. We hold

ourselves back from SO MUCH because of fear.

Please answer the following question:

**Do you deserve to be successful?** yes !

What was your first quick answer just now? What

came flashing into your mind as you read that?

If you answered to yourself, "Heck, YEAH, I do!"

then that's awesome. You're ready to conquer

these digital stages.

But if ANY part of your mental chatter went

something like, "Ummm….welllll….er,...maybe..."

Or "Nah….I don't know how to become

successful." Or "I've tried and it never works. I'm a

failure. It'll never happen…" Or "I'm afraid of what

others might think of me if I really go for it…" then

we have some work to do.

Believe it or not, this question and how someone

responds is directly tied to someone's success on

going Live and whether or not I see them staking

their territory and grabbing as much land as possible

right now to grow their business.

After interviewing about 250 entrepreneurs asking

them why they aren't going Live to grow their

business (especially when they see others doing it

right alongside them), I found the same few answers over and over.

"I don't like the way I look." "I'm too old." "I don't know how and don't know what to say." "I've gained weight and don't want people to see me on camera." "I'm way too busy." "People will think I'm doing too much and being braggadocious or just wanting attention."

But after I dug deeper and asked more personal questions, those were just excuses they used to keep them "safe." And to keep them out of the spotlight that is required to find success.

**Most people haven't given themselves permission to step into the spotlight.**

And why not? Because it's SCARY!

They're afraid of being too visible, of being too exposed or of potential failure and mistakes made and possible judgement from others who might be watching.

Or, they're actually afraid that it's REALLY gonna work and they won't know how to handle all of that success because it's unchartered waters, so they just avoid going there in the first place.

It's way more familiar and comfortable to stay

broke when that's all someone has known.  Just

keeping it real.


All of these thought processes are SUPER common.

We're our own worst critic and the negative

self-talk can be terrible.  Family dynamics and

upbringings can sometimes be the biggest hurdle to

jump over in order to live an abundant and

richly-fulfilling life.


But I'm here to tell you, it's those who believe they

deserve to find success who are crushing it in their

business.  They're confident and don't apologize for

who they are, how they show up and what they have

to offer to the world.

They carry this out when they're broadcasting Live, too. You can see it - and in REAL TIME!

You probably can picture someone you've seen going Live on Facebook and crushing it right now in your head. Who comes to mind when you think of someone in your industry who's SO GOOD at going Live?

When you think of this person, does he/she seem timid and unsure of themselves? Or are they confident and clear about what they're there to do - and what's theirs to take?

Successful people must FIRST believe they can do

it. They must believe they deserve it.

And a lot of the times it's not necessarily your fault if you've been taught things like "money is the root of all evil" or "rich people are mean and selfish" when you're desperately trying to break that pattern or cycle and actually make it happen.

There are tremendous books and resources out there that'll help you break through these very limiting beliefs. It takes work but it's totally possible to change your mind. You can DECIDE that these negative thoughts around becoming successful can kiss your boo-tay goodbye cuz it's your YEAR, baby! And yes, you deserve all the success in the world.

Remember when you were in grade school and your

class had an upcoming field trip? Do you remember

how your parents had to sign the Permission Slip

for you to be able to go? Well it's time you signed

your own Permission Slip of Life and get out there

and GO! You're holding yourself back from a

completely different life by staying safe and quiet

and less visible.  The other kids are on the bus

already - you don't want to miss the adventure, do

you?

If I could sign your Permission Slip for you and

things would change, I would! I can help hold your

hand while you're practicing backstage, getting

ready to open the curtain so you can step into your

digital spotlight all confident and feeling awesome,

but I can't force you to be out there if you don't

want to be. It doesn't work that way. This has to

be your decision. And one that you feel sure about

deep down in your gut. No ifs, ands or buts about it

- you DESERVE all the success that's waiting for

you. So sign your slip.

So let's say you've decided to go for it. Great!

**Why do you deserve to be successful?**

How about because you want to leave a legacy? If

you're in business for yourself and identify as an

entrepreneur who sells products or services on your

own (even if you're a consultant or distributor of a company) then you probably have desires to really change your family's future - and do it on your terms, with freedom of time and space flexibility.

*There is SUCH a huge opportunity right now to be a part of a great direct sales company, to build your own company, to establish your personal brand and to grow in business. And to simply CRUSH IT ALL from leveraging these FREE platforms we call social media. This is the winning formula for 2019 and beyond. The old way of doing things can kick rocks.*

Ok, ok. I know I'm up on my soapbox, but the way the Internet is set up for you, my friend...wow. It's perfect timing. RIGHT NOW.  Several of my

mentors and other marketing pros I look up to in

this space agree that this is the best time in the

history of humankind to be an entrepreneur.  Yes,

it'll take work. Nothing comes easy or free. But,

think about the generation before you and how hard

they had to bust their butts every day to make ends

meet - or even to simply communicate.  Can you

imagine the struggle when they had to use the Pony

Express to deliver a message? Imagine doing

business at this pace! Lord, no! We are blessed

today with the speed of which we live to get things

done more efficiently.


Today you have 10-year-olds making millions of

dollars just by opening up new toys on video and

taking them out of the packages. I mean….what the what?!

So if little Johnny can figure out YouTube then I know you can conquer these digital stages, too. And you'll be leaving a legacy for generations to come as that person who cracked the Internet code and set the family up for success.

I believe you also deserve success because by doing so you're setting an amazing example to others. Do you have a team or are there business partners in this endeavor with you? By leading by example, you'll increase the overall team motivation. Your success will inspire others to copy you (instead of that person they found on Facebook who's not entirely doing it right). Let them copy the right cat.

Let them see YOU as the brilliant, shining light that

you are. Even if you're just getting started, I

guarantee you that they're watching you. They're

watching what you do (and what you don't do). So

jump on board. Inspire them. Do this together!


**A special note for my entrepreneurs in a direct**

**sales company or affiliate marketing company**

**who has the opportunity to sell their products by**

**going Live on social media:**


The success of someone in a direct sales or affiliate

marketing company is based on how well they

duplicate an already-proven system. This is one of

the reasons why millions of people are signing up,

getting their Starter Kits and embarking on the "side-hustle and might gon' turn it into my main hustle cuz they got elementary school teachers retiring in their 30s, baby" business.

You see people in your company making a ton of money by going Live. Yes, there are multiple ways to make money in your business, but this particular system and process WORKS. Really well. It wasn't even available until not that long ago! The easiest path to success for YOU, is to duplicate what they're doing.

**Are you a leader of a team? Let's do the math:**

If you don't master going Live, your team won't

follow your lead.

If your team doesn't follow your lead, they'll make less sales.

If they make less sales, you make less commission and you take longer to rank up.

*Going Live is not only something every entrepreneur should learn how to do for their business, but it's ESSENTIAL if you're an Independent Consultant or Distributor in a direct sales company where you're paid more money, and rank up higher and higher based on **your team's results, too.** If going Live to make additional sales is working, do the math with it and do the math* *without it and it'll be so obvious what you need to do.  THIS MAKES LEARNING TO GO LIVE A NO-BRAINER.*

I've never seen a more simple strategy that if you don't figure out how to model it for your team can actually LOSE you potential income like this one. In business terms this would be known as an opportunity cost if you chose to ignore it and not leverage the heck outta this new tool.

**Opportunity cost = Return on the best option not chosen - Return on the option chosen**

Also, let's not forget how amazingly simple and easy selling products on a Live broadcast can be.

Vendor events and parties in someone's home are great! But on a Live broadcast, your team member doesn't have to pack up all their inventory and leave the house, pay a vendor fee, drive to a location, set up tables and displays and signage and have the show then pack it all back up again to take home and unpack.

They simply turn on some lights in the location where their inventory is at the house, and boom! They're in business. Ready to sell.

For this reason alone, you MUST figure this out!

I hope all these reasons have given you more motivation and inspiration to get this thing going. Make the decision RIGHT NOW that you're done playing games and you're ready to build a newer version of who you're called to be.


You got this.

# Chapter Three: Defining Your Personal Brand

If you're the face of your business, or the person
representing the company you sell for, defining
ing your personal brand is one of the most
important things you can do.  If hundreds of
thousands or even millions of other people are
selling the same products at the same price point as
you, then it's even MORE important you learn how
to stand out from the competition.

Defining your personal brand is one of the hardest
things to do because you're so close to who you are.

Everything seems normal and perhaps even, boring.

When I have a new client and we start working

together, I first ask how they would define their

personal brand. Nine times out of ten they get

confused.  I ask them who they are and they say:

there's

"I don't know.  I'm just me.  There's nothing too

exciting about me."

First, I walk them through understanding what a

personal brand is and the various components.

We'll get to that in a bit.  And then I start to dig

deeper and ask more personal questions that really

get them to think and reflect on who they actually

are, what their values are, and what they want to

achieve by showing up in the world.

By this point in your life you've collected a TON of unique and interesting experiences. These experiences might seem just like ordinary life to you, but to an outsider they might seem fascinating. By you going through some things in your life, you're able to speak to and relate to many others. By nature we're a curious species, and letting people get to know you is key to portraying a personal brand and establishing trust - especially when going Live on social media.

The combination of who you are on the inside with the experiences and stories you've lived through, plus the visuals on the outside make up who you are completely. Take components of your story and who you've become, and highlight these in your personal brand to help people learn more about who you are compared to all the others - and why they should like you enough to do business with you.

**Let me share an example of what this looks like.**

During my 11+ years in Los Angeles, I've been lucky to have been a part of Hollywood and the entertainment industry in more ways than one. As a teenager living on a small farm in Illinois, I never thought my life would take me to "Tinsel Town" and I often tell people I've accidentally been on camera throughout my whole career. But I was never much into going to the movies and we didn't

even have a TV set until I was in junior high.

I remember boarding my plane to visit Los Angeles

for the first time back in college.  The guy in line

next to me asked if I was an actress as we waited to

find our seats.

I chuckled in disbelief and said, "No, but, thank

you. I'm flattered."

I was a young, naive, thinner (yeah...aren't we all

thinner in our 20s?!), super ambitious marketing

nerd beginning my social media marketing career,

but I guess people come to their own conclusions by

looking you up and down - especially on a flight
from Chicago to Los Angeles.


Over time, I gathered quite a lot of experiences that
exposed me to what it was like being on set of a TV
show or movie. I've spent the majority of my
career behind the scenes, supporting the people
on-camera through my marketing and social media
strategies. I wasn't ever IN "the biz" of Hollywood,
but it was all around me.


When I worked for Paul Mitchell the School, I was
working with talented hair stylists and makeup
artists whose art just blew me away with how
they'd transform someone in their chair. I created
opportunities for them to showcase their work and

gain more experience on reality TV shows,

photoshoots, runway fashion shows, modeling

campaigns, movies and more.

I love the energy of people bustling around

backstage. Models, producers, directors, sound

people, lighting people. To get everyone ready for

a show takes some work, but wow...the audience

LOVES seeing pretty people look so nicely put

together.

Fast forward several years later and I had an

opportunity myself to be a model (curves and all!)

on "The Queen Latifah Show." Random

occurrences happen like this in a big city of

opportunity. Corporate marketing chick by day and

curvy model by...day? (Shows tape during the day, typically).

A co-worker who knew I was confident and comfortable in my skin had suggested I send my info to the producers of the show. Not long after, I got a call.

Before I knew it, I was all dolled up and waiting in the green room. I was nervous yet excited. Eventually, someone on the crew came and grabbed me for our segment. After getting my mic attached backstage, it wasn't long before I took my place on stage and the Queen herself was saying my name as the cameras rolled. I was there with her during a makeup segment in front of a live audience and millions of TV viewers. I was excited! The adrenaline was pumping through my veins as I sat there and did my part, trying to remember to breathe.

Side note: I also felt like I was gonna throw up! If you've ever been nervous to be on camera, trust me when I say I know what you're talking about!

The thought that I was the only curvy model there with everyone looking at my chubby face, the thought of not saying the right things and messing up on national TV made me so nervous, but I made it through. For those of you who've seen me on video before this, you probably wouldn't believe that even *I* get nerves. But it's true, AND I'm here to tell you that if I can do this, you can, too! It gets easier and easier the more you do it.


I'm super grateful for that experience. It was during this random taping of a TV show where I got my signature #CurvyHipsRedLips look! Out of the three models, her celebrity makeup artist, Sam Fine, chose me to showcase how to rock a red lip. Whew! That was hot fire, baby. I loved the look and felt like a million bucks! I remember all of the compliments that people gave me backstage and hugs after we were done. The adrenaline was still kicking, too, and it felt like a complete endorphin high. So amazing to "perform" on stage, as myself, in front of a Live audience!

After we wrapped the filming of the show (we were done before lunch), I changed out of my fancy designer dress and back into regular business casual clothes, drove the ten minutes from the Sony Studios lot and went right to my office in Santa Monica.  I remember asking my boss for a personal day but we had finished early, so I went right to work, optimizing Facebook Ads and managing the company's social media.

A few hours later a co-worker stopped by my desk for something and did a big double-take.

"Whoa!" he said.  "Where have YOU been today?"

I had totally forgotten that I was wearing regular clothes but that I was still rockin' a bold, bright red lip and a face full of camera-ready makeup.

He taught me a lesson that day - something as simple as lipstick made people take notice.

The red lips have stuck with me ever since and rarely do you see me on a video or in pics without some lipstick on. (Btw, lipstick comes off, but my curves will always be here, no matter what size I am.  And that's ok!)

I share this story with you because we have different parts of who we are, during different times and circumstances.  It's when we reflect back and realize some pivotal moments that helped shape who we are today that we can help define our personal brand.

We also like to change things up. A red lip is definitely part of my personal brand but not all the time. Don't feel like you have to be "camera ready" 24/7.

Monday through Friday I typically wear business casual clothes, or jeans and a nice shirt, basic makeup. On the weekends I'm in yoga pants and workout clothes, comfy. Not a stitch of makeup.

And then sometimes I'm preparing to be on camera and it's hair did, makeup did, everything did!

Accessories to die for, of COURSE! At that point I'm in "hair, makeup and wardrobe," as they call it in Hollywood. I'm preparing to present something to an audience, even if just one person were to tune in, but that's my personal brand.

I'm the same Kerianne in all of those scenarios, but I definitely put more effort into what my personal brand *looks like* when I'm creating content for anything online.

Ladies, I encourage you to do the same.

Now, am I saying you need to hire a Glam Squad to do your hair and makeup every time you're about ready to go Live? No, I'm not. Although if you had the free service offered to you, wouldn't you take

it? I KNOW I WOULD! #goals

**Let's break down a few basic principles that you**

**should know about marketing and business.**

1.  Everyone likes looking at nice things.  This

includes people!

2.  It takes 7 seconds for someone to see you and

make a decision about you.

3.  The more polished, put-together and professional

you appear, the higher your perceived value will be.

This carries over into the products that you're trying

to sell.

Imagine a shopping experience on Rodeo Drive in Beverly Hills - everything proper and perfect, in its place. Glamour and sophistication. Fashion and style. Elegance and appeal.

Now imagine shopping at Wal-Mart the day after Black Friday and no one has straightened up the shelves. Messy and chaotic. Disorganized and ugly. Not a good look.

For the record, I've experienced both of those scenarios and at a younger age I actually was one of the Wal-Mart employees who had to straighten out the Shoe Department the day after that crazy shopping bonanza. I'm grateful for my humble beginnings and have fond memories of years of

hard work in retail. :)


The point is, there's a more appealing experience.
And regardless of the pricepoint of your products
for sale, it still matters how it's all presented. You,
included. We'll get to the total presentation a bit
later, but understand that YOU are going to be the
main focus of any Live broadcast.


In general, I want you to realize some basic
concepts and start thinking about how you see
yourself as you develop your strategy for going
Live on social media:


**Digital Stage**: a place where you "perform" in front

of and with an audience (ie - Facebook, Instagram, YouTube, etc)

**Audience**: your followers & friends (ie - business partners, mentors, friends from high school, an old neighbor you reconnected with 25 years later, random strangers and people checking you out because one of those people just shared your video)

**Performance:** the "show" you give the audience on social media (ie - a Facebook Live, a pre-recorded video or mini-commercial, a written post, a super cute selfie)

All of these things mimic Hollywood and if you think about it, you're kinda doing the same exact things.  The audience is watching you.  They don't

have to be there, and we already covered how many

alternative choices (or "channels") they have to

watch instead of you.  They can easily click out of

your video and leave to keep scrolling.

Once you capture people's attention in the

Newsfeed, it's up to you to keep it.

**So how do you figure out what your personal**

**brand looks like?**

The winning formula for a strong personal brand

online:

*Confidence + Authenticity + Personality =*
*SUCCESS*

The three components listed above help your

audience get to know you, like you and trust you.

And when they trust you, they give you their credit

card information to purchase products or services

from you. This is success. This is the goal, my

friend!


Let's break down what each of these means further.


1. CONFIDENCE is key.

Go back to thinking about that person you watch on

Facebook Live who's crushing it. Are they

confident? I don't even know who you're thinking

about and I already KNOW that person is confident.

Confidence is attractive. (A smile is the cherry on

top.) We're really drawn to someone on camera who looks comfortable and who enjoys what they're doing. Confidence is an inside job and if you have to psych yourself up before you turn on the camera to go Live, then do it. Fake it til you make it, baby.

Take deep breaths and repeat *"I got this! I'm amazing and confident and I'm going to have a blast just being myself on here as I do my thing."*

Bonus tip: Confidence grows over time. It's like a seed that needs watering, though. Keep at it. Give it water and sun. You'll blossom pretty quickly. Decide you're awesome and then believe it.

2. Authenticity is key.

When I first started streaming Live online many years ago, I thought I had to portray a different character of myself. A different, more professional version of myself. Well, let me tell you what I've learned over and over - the more REAL I was on video, the more RESPONSE and ENGAGEMENT I got from the audience. I've also made more money, the more real and authentic I am. You'll inspire others to work with you if you give yourself permission to just be yourself.

Plus, we live in a time and age where people are dying for transparency. The "keep it real" concept is not only a wish, but a demand from consumers.

Gone are the days of brands hiding behind PR campaigns. Since you're a *personal* brand, not a *corporate* one, it's totally ok for you to just keep it real. Show up and be 100% authentic. People will trust you (and therefore, get out their credit cards or say "Invoice me!" that much quicker).

3. Your PERSONALITY is key.

Some of the best entrepreneurs going Live on social media stand out easily. Everyone who's crushing it, in my opinion, does one of two things:

1) Makes you laugh, or

2) Makes you think.

They're either entertaining or informative, but it's their personalities that capture and KEEP your attention.

Think about the characters you see on your favorite reality TV shows. They're people, human, with real names and families...but Hollywood literally calls them "characters." And yes, some shows will document some of these characters being super extra, flipping tables or acting a fool, but it's no mistake that MILLIONS of people are drawn to reality TV shows for the entertainment value.

While this entertainment value is defined differently by each of us (there's quite a range of preferences between "Keeping Up with the Kardashians" and

"Duck Dynasty"), I encourage you to start thinking

about what kind of "character" you are when you

appear on video. What type of personality do you

have?

Am I going to ask you to morph into someone that

you're not? Nope. I actually want you to become

the most authentic form you can be. (Remember

step #2 above)

I tell my clients who are timid or shy or more

reserved to find that energy they have when they're

out with their girlfriends on a Saturday night and

channel that. Or maybe it's game night at the house

with a few other couples and friends. Your fun and

entertaining personality comes out then, so I know

it's in you!

For the record, not everyone who's a "character"

with a really bold personality wakes up in the

morning and is on 10...ready to be on camera that

moment.  No, this isn't realistic.  But when they

know they have to "perform", the step up their

game a bit.

That's what I'm asking you to do, too.  Step up your

game.  Bring up your personality and energy several

notches and you'll be ready to have a great Live

broadcast.

Keep in mind that if you've had a long day at work

and you're grumpy or super tired and your energy is low, I'd rather you waited until you felt up to the task and just not go Live at all. Don't forget that it takes hard work just to CAPTURE someone's attention in the Newsfeed, let alone keep it. Make sure you're mentally prepared to do your best every time. Stay consistently amazing.

Take some time and write down a description of who you are:

What is your personal brand? What do you look like? What do you sound like? What is your style? What do you like to share or talk about with your audience? What is unique and special about you? What experiences have shaped you into the person you are today? How are you known by your close

circle of family and friends?

A key to doing this exercise correctly is to look at

your list of answers and ask yourself, "Does this

specifically define ME? Or could I swap out

someone else's name and it'd work for them, too?"

Being "nice" or "friendly" is different than "I

volunteer every quarter at the homeless shelter to

give back to our community" or "I never let an old

person struggle with opening a door." Get specific.

Your mission, my friend, is to dig deep and find

those super special parts of you. Once you're aware

of all your awesomeness, you'll feel more confident

to step out onto your digital stages and let others get

to know you, too.

# Chapter Four: The #1 Biggest Mistake You Can Make while Going Live on Social Media

Believe it or not, this mistake is not about saying the wrong thing, wearing the wrong outfit, not looking presentable, having a distraction happening outside of the camera's frame (or inside it) you didn't intend for people watching to see….nope. None of that.

Have you ever heard of the saying in business "ABS?" It stands for "always be selling."

As an entrepreneur or someone in business, your goal is to make money. Considering you didn't start a hobby or you aren't running your biz like a non-profit, you would be wise to keep your eyes on the money prize. This mentality of an "always-on" to make money mindset is helpful, HOWEVER, we must be very careful where and how we apply this strategy.

If you are the face of your business and relationships matter to you, the #1 biggest mistake you can make while going Live on Social Media for your business is to ALWAYS BE SELLING.

The quickest way to get someone to unfriend you,

unfollow you, un-"Like" your Facebook Page, ignore you or the worst, BLOCK YOU, is to always be selling on social media. If they wanted a firehose of non-stop commercials they'd be watching QVC or Home Shopping Network, not scrolling through Facebook or Instagram.

I'm speaking mostly to your personal friend's timelines, not Facebook Business Pages or Groups, but tell me I'm wrong if you can't think of an entrepreneurial person right now on your friend's list who is working your very last nerve cuz 100% of all of their posts are salesy. All they do is ask for you to buy from them and support their business each time they post on Facebook or Instagram. I bet you come up with several people, actually. I know I do! The direct sales industry is notorious for this and it's my mission to help people avoid the pitfalls and learn some social selling etiquette.

Let me break this down further.

1. Social Media platforms are meant for being *social* first, not commercial. Look at the first word again in "social media."

2. You CAN sell on these platforms, yes, but you must first understand and respect what the platform is intended to be used for and how you fit into that picture.*

3. You must apply relationship building, marketing, branding AND sales strategies to build a successful business. Not just the last one.

4. At the end of the day, your sales increase the more relationships you build with people who know, like and trust you.

*Facebook, IG, etc have rules on where and how you can sell and it's constantly evolving (and/or the enforcement of these rules is also changing frequently). Be sure to read the Terms & Conditions to be aware of any restrictions or potential roadblocks when selling on social media. Also, be aware of your company's policies and procedures as they may have restrictions that*

*Compliance Departments just haven't been able to*

*enforce across the board.*

If you understand these four essential rules, then
you're golden.

I see TOO many people as I scroll through my
timelines on Instagram and Facebook who are
always selling, 100% of the time.  The only reason
they come on is to sell, sell, sell.

Since I love you and want you to succeed (and I
also don't want you getting shut down or put in
Facebook jail), I want you to catch this next part
with the deepest level of understanding that you can
muster.

*If you don't figure out how to add value to your audience, they'll have little patience for sticking around and checking out your posts.*

*If your posts and videos are only about sales and your business, you're training your audience to know you as someone who's only going to ask for their money. Every. Single. Time. You do not want this!*

This is a book about learning how to go Live on social media, but if you think it's ONLY purpose is to sell, sell, sell then I ask you to keep an open mind. Going Live on Facebook or Instagram has many different purposes. It's a multi-dimensional tool in your business toolkit.

Over my 14+ years experience in social media marketing, I've seen this work over and over again…

**The secret sauce of learning to go Live to take your business to the next level is to use it for MANY reasons, not just to sell!**

In short, you must give your audience something of value.  Switch it up every now and then!

I've created some ideas to help you brainstorm what other types of Live broadcasts you can do beside just be selling (aka turning people off or burning them out after seeing all your sales-y videos).

Let's say you're in the fashion business and you sell beautiful accessories. Aside from your dedicated jewelry shows where you show people inventory and they comment on which pieces they want to purchase from you, these are alternative ideas.

When I work with my clients on developing a deeper part of their overall social media content strategy, they hear the strategy of "make people laugh more!" and think I'm requiring them to all of a sudden turn into a stand-up comedian, go Live, and give their audience a 30-minute show. No! That's not required. But if you recall from earlier, the idea is to have you capture people's attention, stop them from scrolling in the Newsfeed, be yourself, but keep them interested. That could mean something as simple as you going Live and recalling something funny that happened to you today. Or you could go deeper and research the recent People's Worst Dressed list and talk about the terrible wardrobe decisions made by celebrities and their stylists. To kick it up a whole other notch, find clothes YOU wish you didn't purchase, model them on camera and talk about fashion do's and don'ts while being funny and entertaining. Wear some coordinating jewelry you have in your inventory for subtle hints that you are "the jewelry lady/man." You won't be selling, but you'll be planting seeds.

For instance, as a Consultant in the beauty brand

industry you might be the person who goes Live to

talk about the newest collaboration of makeup

products with a celebrity and a major makeup

brand. Share pricing, where they can find it, which

of the products you'd want to try, etc. Since the

topic goes hand in hand with what you sell, your

audience will take interest. You're positioning

yourself as the expert in this area and providing

extra value to them. They'll appreciate you for this!


When you master the overall strategy of going Live

to build relationships with people who will

eventually (or continue) to buy from you by not

always trying to move your inventory, you're

setting yourself up for success. Avoid selling all the

time, care more about what's in it for your

*customers* and not yourself, and you'll be winning.

# Chapter Five: The S.T.A.R. Strategy - The "S": Set Up Your Stage

Now that we've covered the mindset part of going Live as well as the overall marketing outlook on what kind of content you need to create during your Live broadcasts, you're ready for the more technical "know-how" of how to go Live.

After doing hundreds (maybe even thousands) of my own Live broadcasts on platforms from UStream to Periscope to Facebook Live to

Instagram Live, plus having a look for several years at those who are also live streaming for business purposes, I realized there are four main keys to success. I took those observations and created the "S.T.A.R. Strategy" to help keep it simple and streamlined. If you master all of these components in addition to defining your own personal brand, you'll be a legit STAR out there on your digital stages!

The first part of the **STAR Strategy is "S."** The "S" stands for:

Set up your stage.

There are many different components of this first part and they all have to do with the visuals.

1.  Lighting
2.  Hair, Makeup, Wardrobe
3.  Frame
4.  Background

The first category we'll tackle is your LIGHTING.

In my "10 Commandments of Facebook Live" the First Commandment is "Thou shall be lit. Like, literally. #lightingiseverything"

When I've been on sets of movies or TV shows the most obvious difference between that space and the "real world" (besides the fake walls and rooms) is all the extra lights! Hanging from the ceiling above, standing all over the floor of the set hidden off-camera, from the front, the side...all over. I've even worked behind the scenes on a movie that we shot at night, in the middle of nowhere, in the Redwoods of Northern California. Surrounded by the giant trees, the lighting department brought in HUGE lights to get that forest lit! If you're shooting something on camera but it's hard for your audience to make out what it is, then you're leaving money on the table.

Even during the day with access to sunlight on most productions, there's still allll kinds of lights added to brighten up the shot - especially on programs such as QVC or Home Shopping Network.  They require great lighting to showcase products that the hosts are trying to sell to the viewing audience.

As the face of your business, bringing in extra light for your Live video strategy is KEY to helping you and your products look amazing.

If you have a business where you're selling products (especially shiny, sparkly, gorgeous ones) then having the right light is ESSENTIAL to increasing your sales.  If you have a list of things you need to purchase for your business to succeed and can only afford to invest in one of them right now, I'd tell you to pick buying better lighting as the FIRST choice.  It's that critical.

When you add light, several things happen:

1. Your production value instantly goes through the roof! You look WAY more professional.
2. People will take you more seriously. They'll see that you're really making an effort to do this the right way.
3. You'll look younger. Not kidding.

The last one might blow your mind but it's a known fact that ring light kits have made average-looking people turn into supermodels just by flipping on that switch! Without extra light behind the camera you're using, you're relying on the light wherever you are. Most people are using dining rooms or living rooms or bedrooms to go Live so they're using the overhead light or a lamp nearby. While this gives you light, it also gives you shadows. Shadows highlight the dark places on your face. In addition, most lights are positioned overhead. That casts light *down* and you really need light shining straight on your face. By adding a bright light kit, it instantly removes shadows, making you look younger and more fresh-faced!

Celebrity makeup artists began this "selfie glam ring light" craze many years ago on YouTube. They realized how effective filming makeup tutorials were for their audience and they would film using a ring light kit to really showcase their products and what they were demonstrating. The ladies looked so beautiful! While knowing how to do your makeup is helpful in looking super put-together, it was the light kit that did a lot of the work.

*Bonus tip: Use a ring light kit for an extra cool effect when you're up close to the camera - the white circle of light will reflect in your pupils and make your eyes "pop" by brightening them up! This is awesome for selfies, too, btw...*

There are several lighting options to buy at affordable pricing, too. You can spend a little (a portable, battery-operated clip-on ring light for your phone (around $10) or a larger light kit with filters, a stand, a dimmer switch and a place to hold your

cell phone (around $60-$150+).

Lighting is everything! Get your light right!

## Hair, Makeup and Wardrobe

The Third Commandment is: "Thou shall look

amazing and shall represent thou company (and

thyself) with pride."

You don't need to look like a supermodel or famous

celebrity to have a successful Facebook Live, but

you do need to look presentable.

In the chapter about defining your personal brand, you should have learned what that looks like for you as far as the optics and visuals of how you want to show up in the world when creating content for your social media channels.

Unless your brand is sweatpants or PJs (and if it is, you better ROCK THAT with confidence, consistently!) it's important to have on the right outfit before going Live. What people see of you matters! How you present yourself is a direct reflection of the brand value and experience the audience expects from you. If you're sloppy and careless, that translates into their perception of you as a business person.

I work from home so I'm often dressed in super

comfy clothes.  In fact, if I don't have plans to go

Live and/or work with my private clients on Zoom

video calls that day, I'm usually in t-shirts and

leggings and absolutely no makeup.

My on-camera personal brand, however, is

glamorous! I rock lipstick and makeup and hair...all

hooked up.  I love it and I pull from the knowledge

I learned about hair and makeup from staying up till

3am watching those YouTube makeup tutorials,

plus the experience of working in the beauty

industry and being around hair and makeup artists

in Los Angeles.  Doing my hair and makeup and

picking out clothes is also part of my artistic outlet

in a very business-driven day of mine.  It's

important for me to have balance. I encourage you
to look at this part of getting "camera-ready" as an
act of self-love and fun creativity in addition to a
business strategy.

You can go Live on your phone and be mobile, so
let's chat about what this looks like when you're not
prepped for a show in your home "studio." If I'm
out somewhere and the Live broadcast is
spontaneous and I'm *not* all made up but I want to
go Live, then I make the adjustments that I can and
provide context of my environment to the audience.
Just be mindful that you're creating trust by
showing up consistently, and caring about your
overall presentation is part of building that trust. I
carry several different red lipsticks in my purse just

for this reason alone.  Backups, ready!

*An important side note for my friends selling*

*jewelry, clothes, makeup, accessories or other*

*products in the beauty or fashion industries:*

You're the group of people who help others watch

to look and feel good about their appearance.  If

your appearance isn't together, something's off -

and the audience can tell.  It's a subliminal message

that your offer doesn't match your values and it

makes people question you.  Not good! However, if

you look like a million bucks your audience will

instantly be drawn to you right away.  The chances

of them sticking around longer to see what products

you have to sell them are higher, and this, therefore,

helps increase your sales volume!

If you're showing jewelry up close to the camera and your painted nails are broken or chipped, then that's the visual you're giving your audience about how much you care about your appearance. Subliminally, it could lower the perceived value of the items you're trying to sell. Your goal is to MAKE sales, not lose them, right? I understand sometimes life gets too hectic to make a last-minute nail appointment, but do what you can to plan in advance and look your best before going Live.

As much as I appreciate finding your inner confidence to be your authentic self, the outside visuals matter here. It's not so much about vanity,

but it's definitely about a psychological need for
your viewer to want to stay and watch. People like
watching people who are put together. It's just a
fact. So use these tips to present yourself in a way
that makes you look absolutely fabbbbbbbulous,
dahling!

**Your Frame**

When an actor is filming a TV show, movie or
commercial, the "shot" and what's inside the frame
of the camera lens is what the audience sees. The
Director and camera person work together to frame
up precisely what they want to show. If the camera
were to spin around, you'd most likely see the parts
they *don't* want you to see! For instance, the rest of

the pretend house or the fake room they've built for

the scene.  You'd see the rest of the crew, maybe

people running around in the background getting

things ready for what's next on camera in between

takes.

When I was a makeup model on "The Queen

Latifah Show" I loved seeing the entire sound stage

filled with multiple sets that included couches and

chairs and other talk show setups for all the various

segments.  Multiple cameramen and sound guys and

producers and such were right there next to the

cameras, but you couldn't see them if you were

watching at home.

When getting ready to go Live, I want you to think

Learn to Go LiveMellott | 118

of your camera's screen as your frame - just like the folks using a camera to shoot a TV show, movie or commercial. What your audience sees (and what they *don't* see) matters a lot here. Become aware of what appears on screen.

For instance, if you work from home and you're setting up your camera on a tripod on a desk in your bedroom, can we see the pile of dirty laundry behind you on the floor? Or is your camera's frame moved slightly to the left so it's out of the frame and we see your bed, neatly made instead? If you're set up in the kitchen, is your camera's frame showcasing the pile of dirty dishes in the sink or the mess on the table? Are you highlighting the pile and stacks of papers and bills and boxes and the garbage can and random things on the couch way in the background of the shot? Take a look around before you begin.

So why does this matter, you ask?

When a viewer first clicks through to watch your video, they see everything. They size you up (and the environment) within seconds. SECONDS! They make instant computations about who you are.

If fear of what others might think of you is already something you're dealing with, fixing these things is a way to help yourself appear more professional, credible and legit.

Also, if you're asking people to share your video, there's a good chance someone completely new to you might click through and join your broadcast (or check out your encore recording).  All the more reason to be on point every single time so you can make a great first impression! You only get one shot at that.

Recent studies say that people create a judgement of who someone is within a nanosecond of first seeing you.  That's QUICK, my friend.  Your environment and what is shared is part of that assessment. They're looking to see if you're trustworthy and competent.  In a business relationship, your ability to fulfill your intentions is everything.

So let's say you've adjusted your camera's frame and the laundry and dirty dishes are out of sight. The next piece of advice is critical to your success!

*Where you position yourself on camera makes a big difference - especially if you're selling products.*

As I scroll through my Facebook Newsfeed, I see this huge mistake all too often - someone's trying to sell jewelry but their beautiful pieces of bling are completely hidden by the comment section!

If you go Live using your cell phone (which I recommend) and it's in Portrait Mode (which is tall and vertical and standing up and down the long way) then you have to be aware of how the comments on your broadcast show up on the screen. The way Facebook is set up currently, comments from your viewers take up about the bottom 50% of the screen. Therefore, if you have beautiful things you're selling and you aren't positioned to show them higher above that part, then you reduce your chances of people buying your products.

Imagine you were watching a HSN or QVC program and they showed products they were selling but they were hidden behind the graphic on-screen showing the product number, pricing information, etc. Ooops. Instant drop in sales. Also, it's possible, but rarely will someone keep swiping the comments away to view your whole screen, then bring them back on screen all throughout your show, so keep this in mind. The worst case scenario - the person watching gets frustrated because they can't see so they CHANGE THE CHANNEL. This is really bad if they leave! Be conscientious of where you and your products are showing up.

*Bonus tip: In Advertising, there's a phrase called "above the fold." Back in the day when there was no TV or social media, newspapers carried the important information of the day. The most valuable and newsworthy stories were always "above the fold." Newspapers are folded in half, so whatever made it above the fold was seen by more people, and was seen first. I translate this concept using a camera to communicate with your audience the same way.*

*If you're going Live on a mobile phone in Portrait Mode, take up the top half of the screen - "above the fold." Try to position your head right underneath the top of the frame. Let the less important things on camera fall below that halfway mark.*

*Bonus, BONUS TIP: If you're on camera, it's daytime and there's a WINDOW anywhere in your frame, take caution. The bright light behind you from the window usually wins and you become dark and hard to see. Your camera is going to pick up that light. Instead, move your camera so the window is out of the frame. Or, FACE the window and use the natural light to brighten you up.*

*Sometimes I see FB Lives and it's sooooo bright*

*behind them from the window's light that it's very*

*distracting to watch and I usually leave.*

Are you ready for the tips on how to look younger

and thinner in seconds? This is my favorite part.

You've probably heard the phrase "the camera adds

10 pounds." When I tell you I see people's Live

broadcasts and they look WAY bigger than they are

in real life simply because of where they place their

camera, I just want to climb through my screen and

adjust their phone! It's like the sticker thingie you

see on a side mirror of a car that says: "Objects in

mirror appear larger than they are"...or something

like that.  False advertising! You are not that big.

Here's how to avoid this:

If you can look almost directly straight into the lens of your camera, you're good.  If you have to look down at all, you've successfully gained weight that you actually don't have on your body.  Angles are everything, my friend! If your camera lens is way down below your eye level, your audience is looking UP at you (and possibly seeing a double or triple chin that you don't actually have).

Now, if you're moving around a lot, the key would be to still have your camera at eye level or a little above your eye level so your head is still near the top of the frame and you're not selling the ceiling (or the sky).

Using all of the concepts in this section will have you looking like a pro in no time! Setting up your digital stage to look as professional as possible will not only be pleasing to your audience's eye, but it will help you increase your sales. Give these helpful tips a try!

# Chapter Six: The S.T.A.R. Strategy - The "T": Talk with Your Audience

One of the most frequently asked questions I get from people who are thinking about going Live on social media is, "What am I supposed to talk about? I'm afraid I'll get on there and just go blank, or worse, not be interesting enough and have no one watching me."

Well, my friend, if this is your thought as well then you'll love this section of the book! I'll show you strategies to make this super easy for yourself.

The "T" in the S.T.A.R. Strategy stands for:

Talk with Your Audience.

Let's refer back to the #1 biggest mistake you can
make when using social media for business - *to
always be in selling mode.* Don't do that!

I understand that business is about making sales but
it's first about building relationships.
ESPECIALLY on social media.

When you first start out, find yourself some
amazing free platforms to build a profile, Page,

Group, etc, set up shop and offer your products or

services. However, there's gotta be a balance in

order to offer real value to your audience in order to

get them even into the *consideration* phase of

purchasing from you.

Just as a reminder, your friends don't grab their

phones along with their credit card each time they

log in to check their Facebook notifications or start

scrolling through the 'Gram, right? Nope. While

they jump on Facebook or Instagram real

quick...while they chill on the couch or in the break

room at work or in the kid pickup carpool lane at

school...their credit card is just chilling in their

wallet. It's a social place to gather, not a store,

necessarily. It's your job to switch them into a

buyer's mindset while they have their phone in their

hand.

One of the downfalls of business owners on social

media is to only be thinking about themselves and

what *they* need:

- They need more sales

- They need more customers

- They need more business partners or people

  to join their team

- They need people to know about their new

  products

- They need to advance to the next level so

  they can make more money

- And on and on…

While all of those things may be true and necessary

to become successful in business, the key is to

recognize that none of that happens anyways if you

don't make people happy by serving some sort of

need *they* have.

What I want to share next is going to be another

magical part of you finding success on social media

when going Live.

If you're hearing me say "don't always be selling"

then you're probably wondering what *else* you

could be talking about when you go Live. Before

you start freaking out and feeling overwhelmed that

you need to make up your own talk show, it's easier
(and more fun) than you might think.

Using a tool like Facebook or Instagram Live is just
that - a TOOL. That means you can use it for many
different things to accomplish many different
intentions. Think of it like a gardening tool that
helps grow multiple types of things you can plant in
a garden. When you tend to them all, you can
eventually harvest! Excellent.

Next, I'm going to break down the two very
important types of broadcasts to help you
understand what type of content you need to talk
about with your audience. The goal is to have a nice
balance of selling *and* adding value to their time

spent with you.

**Two Types of Broadcasts:**

1. Runnin' and Gunnin'

2. Ready and Rehearsed

Runnin' and Gunnin'

Humans are smart. Before we dive into details, I need you to understand what's *actually* happening when you watch another person who is Live on camera. It's a lot of human behavior and psychology.

In a nutshell, you're able to determine whether or

not they are real because there's no editing.  It's not

pre-recorded, changed around, re-done and

uploaded long after filming.  There's no mask on the

person. It is them in their most vulnerable state

because it is Live in real time.

The majority of communication is nonverbal. So we

watch facial expressions, body movement.  We also

listen to the tone of their voice, the pace of their

speech, their eye contact with the camera and

whether or not they appear confident.  All of that

helps us understand whether or not - and here's the

big thing - we *trust* them or not.

Many things are taking place in any given sales

transaction.  Typically there's a 3-step process a

potential buyer of yours must go through before they hand you their credit card information:

1.  They have to KNOW you.

2.  They have to LIKE you.

3.  They have to **TRUST** you.

This is known as the Know-Like-Trust factor. If those three things have to happen before you get the credit card and the last one is **trust**, Facebook Live is a powerful way to speed you through that process simply from the very fact that you can NOT edit yourself in real-time. It is what it is. You are who you are. They get what they get. Potential customers don't need that much time to make their decision about you!

Establishing their trust in you is important because their brains want to feel safe in a purchase transaction. After all, we're talking about someone giving you access to their money!

You can tell really quickly when someone's being authentic or not. So that's the power. And people will see you when you are broadcasting Live. I don't mean they'll be looking at you, I mean they'll be *seeing* you. And whether you are warm and genuine, or crazy and entertaining. If you're being 100% your authentic self you're going to build these relationships and establish the fact that you're trustworthy with people that you don't even know are watching you.

You're going to be able to inspire them, you're

going to be able to motivate them, maybe educate or

entertain them. You're actually building a

relationship with them and sometimes they never

even comment. They'll watch the encore

presentation and never leave a word. But they keep

coming back and watching your content and little

do you know - one day you'll get a message from

someone who's loved watching your Lives, and it'll

say:


"Hey there! I've been watching your videos.

They're so fantastic….how can I find out more

about what you have going on?..."

And you'll just smile and think to yourself, "What? Where'd you come from?" because that's how powerful it is.

Now if you're feeling overwhelmed or if you're feeling anxious about having to go Live on camera and broadcast yourself with no filters, with no edits, just you, this next part is going to help you understand more about your plan and what you need to record when you do go Live. What you need to say and how you need to say it is part of conquering your digital stage.

Before I break it down into more detail about what "Runnin' and Gunnin'" versus "Ready and Rehearsed" looks like for you strategically, I want to take a heavy burden off of your shoulders with this next concept. Business owners and solopreneurs who are wearing multiple hats are always so happy to hear it because most people that I talk to are feeling overwhelmed with their business. They have so much to do. The marketing seems vast and never-ending. And the social media profiles that they live on never shut off because it's always on, 24/7.

When you're thinking: What should I create? What kind of video series should I make? What should I be talking about? How do I say what? What do I say when there's no one watching? How long should the video be?.... all of these questions on how you create content can get very overwhelming.

Have no fear! You are not a major television network. You are not a major news network. You are not a show with a million dollar budget with lights and crews and cameras. It's going to be okay for your people to watch you on Facebook Live and not expect the moon. Now if you want your own show on Facebook Live (or Facebook Watch, for example), if you want to go to the next level and have a fully produced, different camera angles, a crew on set, hair, makeup, lighting...the whole Hollywood thing, then that's fantastic. But for most small business owners, I'm teaching the type of format where you're able to accomplish your goals just by showing up every now and then with a solid strategy, some good light and good content.

The concept is taken from a long-time mentor of mine and social media genius, Gary Vaynerchuk. One of my clients hired him to speak to her small group of women entrepreneurs way back in 2010. We both gave talks about social media that day and he covered many things, but the most important was the type of content to create. Not much has changed a decade later and his theory remains the same.

He encourages people to just simply document what they're already doing. There's no need to create new things from scratch.

Document what you do. Don't create something new!

You don't need a fully-fledged original programming calendar, minute by minute of every day knowing exactly what's going to happen, what shows are happening and when. That's not for you. That's too much pressure. So instead, if you document your life as either a service-based business, or someone who sells products, you're literally just showing yourself on camera as the person who is delivering the service or the product. The idea is to document your daily life when appropriate, instead of creating all this extra special, new and fancy content.

For instance, I was talking to a husband and wife couple who own an HVAC company in Atlanta. Their world consists of servicing customers with their heating and air conditioning needs. When we were brainstorming content strategies on how to grow their audience on social media, I asked them what a typical day might look like. The husband shared that one of his most favorite things to do is check on his elderly customers to make sure they're warm in the winter. The customer will book a service appointment, and he sits and talks with them and makes them feel comfortable. I bet seeing him is the highlight of their whole week. I suggested he jump on a Facebook Live after he's done with that type of an appointment. Go Live walking up to the van (show that logo and contact info on the side!), get in and then share with his audience the story of

a lovely elderly lady and the story she just shared

from back in the day. In addition, he can be telling

his audience to check in on their elderly family

members and to give him a call if they're in the

local area when they need any service done. He's

engaging, is an expert in his field and truly cares

about his business and their customers. I'd watch

it...and give my grandma a call, too. Boom! He

added value and slightly promoted his business, but

wasn't selling. That's how you do it.


People that we like to watch on social media are just

being themselves. Not a TV show, not a movie

that's all produced and rehearsed. The people that

we like to watch and follow on social media are just

"doing their thing" and sharing what the behind the

scenes of their day looks like. Most of these people

are called influencers.

I would love for you to think of yourself as an

influencer in your field. Isn't that the goal? To get

people to get to know you so you can influence

them in purchase decisions? And they get to know

you by watching you and what you're doing. A very

easy way to reduce the overwhelm is to just

document your life. Don't create all kinds of extra

special content and pretend like you need to have it

on some huge level. Every now and then, sure, and

we could further talk about your specific content

strategy that you can make - especially when it

comes to running paid Ads on social media using

video content. That's fine. But I'm talking about

what's going on behind the scenes in your life. What

is something that we can watch from you that

makes you a human being? What is something that

we can watch from you that makes us trust you, that

makes you relevant to us, that makes you look

normal and relatable? Maybe it's driving to the post

office to drop off customer orders and you go Live

in your car once you arrive there and show the

packages. Maybe it's you cooking dinner for the

kids and you want to share a new recipe that gets

dinner on the table in under 20 minutes because you

have a weekly online meeting with your direct sales

team to get to. That happens to be your everyday

life. How fascinating that your business is

interwoven through your entire days! These are the

moments where I encourage you to think about going Live to let people get to see how amazing (and real) you are.

Both categories of "Ready and Rehearsed" and "Runnin' and Gunnin'" are equally as productive and powerful when it comes to delivering value to your audience. However, "Runnin' and Gunnin'" has a special secret sauce that might have your video go viral! By "viral" it could mean instead of getting 200 views you now have a 1000+ views and climbing which is a lot more than your normal view count! Let me explain how that could happen.

According to UrbanDictionary.com, the definition of 'runnin' and gunnin' means:

"Going all out. In the weeds. Super busy."

Now I *know* you can relate to this, right?! There's always something to be doing in your business and your days can get busy.  However, there are special windows of time throughout your day where something happens, or you're doing something or you're going somewhere or you saw something that is going to inspire you to create content right there. Now that window is only open for a short period of time because when those things happen you are typically more emotionally charged. When you see something, do something, have something, go somewhere that you are excited about or sad about or vulnerable about or shocked about - any sort of

emotion where you're emotionally charged. You're
in prime position to go Live. If you can start
thinking about how to document that experience
and strategically tie it into your business and
position yourself as an influencer it's amazing what
can happen.

Let me give you an example. One time I was at a
business meeting about an hour away from home in
Los Angeles that finished up super late at night. I
stopped to get some quick fast food before making
the trek back. The drive thru was the only thing
open and after I got my food I pulled over to a spot
in a nearby laundromat parking lot.

I looked up and a woman who appeared to be living out of a van saw me. She timidly approached my Mercedes Benz, keeping her distance as to not disturb or scare me. She was in her 30s, I'd guess. She asked me if I had any change that I could spare. She was with her small child and all she wanted was to be able to wash their blanket. Since I was parked outside of a laundromat this made total sense to me. It also broke my heart. I was quick to give her all the change and dollar bills I had on me. She was incredibly grateful and kept saying, "Thank you, ma'am. God bless you! Thank you…"

I was so happy to be able to help and it impacted me in such a way emotionally. It brought me back to my humble beginnings and similar situations of not

having enough money as a single mom when my
son was about the same age. I was living off of
food stamps, and public housing helped us with a
roof over our heads. I got so emotional. She was so
sweet and so polite and so grateful and so thankful.
And after she left to go inside the laundromat I just
broke down.

I was so touched by it emotionally because we all
are here on our journeys. I knew if I could
overcome certain challenges, she could, too. Her
journey could get better and if there's anything I
can do to help instill hope in another woman,
especially, I'm here for it.

Instead of keeping these emotions to myself, I knew
that this was a teachable moment for my audience.
I knew that I wanted to share the experience and I
wanted to give people hope.  I wanted to recall and
connect with those who might not be feeling so
positive about life or their journey or trying this
business or whatever. And so I decide to go Live on
Facebook.

Now, what did that require me to do? First of all,
was I emotionally charged? Yes. My heart was
broken yet hopeful at the same time.  I had tears
running down my face. My eyeliner was starting to
run. I had my full makeup on and it was going to
get messed up. I looked in the mirror real quick as I
contemplated my decision to be super vulnerable

with people.  It was already a little messed up.  I

said, "I don't care. This is so important. I want

people to be inspired and I want people to know that

you can do it. You can make it. I was struggling

once, too. You can get here." That kind of thing.

And so I chose to be brave and I went Live.


There was no business objective at all attached to

this Facebook Live broadcast. It was simply me

giving value to the audience in a short window of

time where I was emotionally charged about a

particular event that had just happened.  An event

where struggle and vulnerability were at the core.

As my stomach continued to growl and my fries got

cold, I paid it no attention because I knew everyone

could relate in some way, shape or form to this
woman's circumstance.

And what were the results? It went viral. So many
people jumped on and shared it while I was Live,
which helped Facebook's algorithm know to send it
out to even more people. More watched the encore
presentation within the next 24 hours. They shared
it, too. They put it on their walls. They tagged their
friends in it. Their friends tagged their friends in it.
And it became this snowball kind of of interaction
and engagement and views just went up - tick tick
tick tick tick tick tick. Thousands of views. And it
was shocking to me. It made me feel two things -
and you'll notice this, too, if you ever put yourself
in this situation.

1. To be vulnerable means you're opening yourself up for judgment. You're opening yourself up for critique. You're opening yourself up for "this is me in my raw human form right now and I have something to say." But guess what? That's ok.

2. It draws humans closer together when they can see someone who is being authentic and real. And when they are that vulnerable and when they are that open and when they're that willing to just put it all out there you actually draw people closer to you. You don't have a mask on when you're on Facebook Live. It's not rehearsed. It's not uploaded and pre-recorded. It's in real time.

And I was having conversations with people

jumping on while I shared what had just

happened, shared part of my story most

people had no clue about, all while choking

back tears. They were offering their

experiences with similar situations. The

comments were blowing up. It just became

an entire movement. And I did not have any

intentions of that happening other than to

know that it was important enough for me to

be as brave as possible in that moment and

be vulnerable and go Live. And that was it.

And sometimes you'll find these moments.


That was a rare moment, filled with an extra dose of

emotion. It doesn't happen every day. But you'll

find windows like that that open up and you can say

to yourself, "OK, this is an opportunity to connect

with my audience."

Now let's say it's not as dramatic as that, you're not

bawling your face off but you are excited about

something. Your client just succeeded in a big, big

way! You just left from seeing them or you're on

your way to them to celebrate a big event and you

want to share that feeling.

Do it. Go Live on Facebook.

Use that window of opportunity when you're

emotionally charged to share with your audience.

It's the most authentic you that you can be.  If you

try to do it later, all the emotion will have been gone
by then and it just won't be as good of a video, trust
me.

I want you to start thinking through your regular
daily activities. How could you turn something
that's happening or just happened into a documented
situation instead of a created and forced situation?
Don't be afraid to embrace your human side, your
connective side. People want to hear from you and
connect with you on a human level. Go ahead and
take advantage of that opportunity using the most
powerful tool you have in your toolbox.

<u>"Ready and Rehearsed"</u>

The name of this second category sounds pretty self-explanatory and, yes, it is a Live broadcast where before you press "three, two, one, go!" and you are Live, you already know what's going to happen. In fact maybe you have a show theme and "set" and your frame is perfectly prepared, you've got your lighting kit, and you're ready to go.   You know exactly what you're going to talk about.  It helps if you're consistent and you show up every Thursday at 12:00 noon or every Friday at 5:00pm, whatever you want to choose. Consistency helps here in establishing trust with your audience.

Examples of a show could mean that you have a guest that you interview once a week. Either you bring them on camera because you can split the screen, or you have them in person with you on camera and you both are taking turns talking. Maybe it's a loyal customer who would love to be showcased or help demonstrate the products you sell. You've already called the guest ahead of time, you've already booked the interview in advance. These are all things that are in your control and can be organized and pre-arranged.

In the next section we're going to talk about how you can make your broadcasts that are "Ready and Rehearsed" really become effective for building your business. We'll brainstorm more ideas on how you can take your time on screen to a whole other

level and get people to not only click through to see

what you're up to but to stay and participate.

# Chapter Seven: The S.T.A.R. Strategy: The "A": Add Value

*"Beauty captures people's attention. Personality keeps it." - Roy R. Gilson*

The third part of the **S.T.A.R. Strategy is "A."** The "A" stands for:

Add value.

If you choose to go Live only to sell to your followers 100% of the time you click that button that says, "3...2...1...",then you're training them that all you want to do is get their money.

If you are selling 100% of the time you go Live,
they'll eventually get the clue this is what you do
whenever you're Live.

Why is this an issue? Well, if they're not in the
buying mood for jewelry or teas or clothes or any
other goods or services that you sell, why would
they join? They have a million other opportunities
for things to take (and keep) their attention instead.
Don't forget that they're finding you going Live
amidst a stream of other posts from their friends and
other Pages they follow.  At any given moment,
every single other post they see is competing for the
attention of their eyeballs. And we're not even
talking about the second screen in the room with

them that is *also* fighting for their attention (usually

a TV, or a tablet - or both!)

When you're scrolling through Instagram or

Facebook's newsfeed your subconscious mind is on

a quest for one thing: to find something that adds

value to your life.  You're looking for someone to

capture your attention with a thumb-stopping post.

Do the same for others who follow you.

The type of content you find valuable on social

media is pretty subjective.  You might find

scrapbooking tutorials really helpful while your

older brother really appreciates muscle car

restoration videos. Your best friend really digs

motivational quotes on Instagram while your mom

loves watching a live-streaming church service in a whole other time zone on YouTube. It's not so much about the content but the value that the viewer sees in it.

When I think about all of the various types of posts that are created and shared on a daily basis, I can break down the end result a viewer is looking for into 3 main categories. This is also a great strategy when it comes to making content - ask yourself if the content you're about to post falls into one or more of the following categories. If the answer is "yes" then proceed with posting. If not, what are you doing? Stop and rethink what you're creating.

**The 3 Categories of Value:**

1. Entertain someone.

2. Inform someone.

3. Educate someone.

Most posts on social media created by people
(non-business people and others) are for
entertainment. Either we're sharing something we
found that's hilarious, interesting, funny, inspiring
or makes us feel good. A lot of this type of content
looks like clips from last night's episode of a really
popular singing competition show where the talent
of the people on this reality show is out of the
world. Or it looks like a friend of yours who goes

Live to share about a funny story that happened to

her on a first date (I've been known to do this

several times!). Either way, you're looking to be

entertained in some way. That brings value to your

life because it helps you calm down from a long

day, or helps you laugh after being stressed about

something, or gives you a feel-good feeling you just

really needed to feel. We live in a world where

everyone loves to be entertained so this brings

immediate value.


The second category of value is all about informing

people about someone, some thing, some place,

some idea, etc. We live in a time and age where we

are bombarded by information. The 24/7 news

cycle is never-ending. Although we also are living

in a day and age where we have access to news and
information at our fingertips, it's impossible to
consume it all by ourselves.  Nobody has time for
that! When someone creates a post that informs us
of something yet helps us save time by just jumping
right in and hearing about a news story, we find this
valuable.  Saving someone time or money are two
key benefits we look for in life and business and by
going Live to inform your followers of something
newsworthy will make you look like a hero and
truly bring value to someone's experience on social
media.

The third category of value is to educate someone.
The key difference between informing like the last
category versus educating is that you bring your

personal experience to the table when you can teach

someone something you, yourself, have actually

learned. Informing is more about just sharing

something you found out about. Educating is taking

ownership of the topic at hand and bringing your

"teacher" hat to the table. Before you think I'm

asking you to turn into your favorite teacher from

elementary school and worry about creating a whole

curriculum, don't freak out and feel overwhelmed.

What I *am* asking you to do is to take some time to

sit and reflect on alllllll the things you actually

know how to do.

We find value in people who educate us and if

there's something you know that you can teach your

audience to make their life better, then be a genius

and use Facebook Live to show them how smart and helpful you are!  You find tons of Facebook Pages/Groups or Instagram profiles that educate their audience on things from how to reclaim furniture from a thrift store, to managing really curly hair, to making easy dinner recipes in 20 minutes or less, to makeup tutorials and more. By teaching skills you've learned throughout your life, you're automatically in a very special category of content producers who are creating exceptional and captivating content. Be strategic and somehow tie in your business by mentioning something about it with what you're doing or teaching about and you're golden.

We tend to get so wrapped up in our day-to-day

lives that we often take for granted what we have

learned over time. In Malcolm Gladwell's book,

"The Outliers," he explains the 10,000 Hours Rule –

the amount of time spent at something until we find

greatness. Are you an entrepreneur or business

owner who had a career for many years doing

something else first? Perhaps you're still working

now at this job and your "side hustle" is

supplementing your income until it's grown enough

to have you quit your job. Either way, you've

probably had some good amount of time under your

belt being proficient in a certain area. Let me give

you an example.

Not that long ago, I was teaching a workshop to a

group of women jewelry entrepreneurs about how

to create their strong personal brand online. The

goal for this was to build an audience of prospective

customers who would buy their jewelry. When I

asked the class what made each of them unique and

special from the hundreds of thousands selling the

same products most of them weren't sure how to

answer me. They thought they were boring and

basic, working 9-5 jobs that most people wouldn't

care much about. So I asked a woman in particular

who was feeling stuck on how to tie her 9-5 job

she'd been doing very well at for 30+ years to tell

everyone what she did for work. Turns out she

works in a hospital and handles all of the tests and

pre-surgery preparations that have to deal with

someone's skin. Apparently, running labs on a

person's skin tells the hospital more about their

health than other (what I thought were more

obvious) tests. So cool! She went on to explain

more about what she does exactly and how she

works with the doctors to provide the best care. As

she continued to talk she got more and more excited

and passionate about her area of expertise. She was

teaching us all the things her labs can screen for and

what they can find.  It was so interesting to listen

to! The whole room thought what she did was

interesting, too. We then worked out ways she

could add value to her FB Live strategy by teaching

people really important things regarding their skin

and health. She asked the room if we thought that

was boring and everyone said, "No! That'd be

really cool to learn more about." I helped her

brainstorm a Facebook Live show where she's able

to tie into her work knowledge with her audience
watching her sell her jewelry.  The point is to make
your broadcasts valuable for your audience, not
yourself.

The three categories of value can also be
intertwined throughout a single Live video
broadcast.  You don't have to pick one category and
stick to that the whole time.  In fact, if you can
incorporate all three into the same "show" then
you'll *really* be looking like a legit professional!
That could look like you deciding to teach your
viewers something but adding humor or a funny
story or anecdote while accomplishing your goal.
The ebb and flow of a Live broadcast varies and if
you're going Live for a long time, you can find

those moments that make sense here and there to keep your audience engaged.

On the contrary, you can add value to your relationships by making shorter Live broadcasts that handle just one of these categories. For instance, my friend told me about his sister and her new baby, his nephew. He's 1 year old and every single day the mom goes Live on Facebook during his mealtime and she gives him different baby food to try out Live on camera. The faces this baby makes when he's NOT PLEASED with a new menu option is beyond cute and quite entertaining. Family and friends know to tune in daily to see his precious reactions.

The extra effort you take by adding value to someone's time shared with you whenever you go Live is WORTH IT.  Stand out from the rest of people going Live on social media and make a difference.  Do the extra work by sharing more of who you are.  Put yourself in the audience member's shoes.  Be remembered as someone who not only cares about entertaining, informing or educating them, but who truly cares about creating a great experience for your audience.

Is it worth it to go that extra mile and claim your spot on the digital stage in order to conquer your fears, reach through the lens, pick up money on the table and grow your business? Most definitely.

# Chapter Eight: The S.T.A.R. Strategy - The "R": Redirect with a Call To Action

We've made it down to the last important step in the 4-step strategy to have an effective Live broadcast. You've learned how to set up your stage, talk to your audience in various ways, add tons of value to keep them coming around and now we need to cover what you want them to do *besides* watch your live broadcast.

The last part of the **S.T.A.R. Strategy is "R."** The "R" stands for:

**Redirect** with a Call to Action.

This is the part where you can reach through the lens and essentially pick up money on the table.

The ability to communicate with your audience in real-time is quite a gift. It's the perfect marketing tool to help share more about who you are and what you have to sell. In traditional marketing and advertising such as TV commercials or radio spots, the advertiser is broadcasting a one-way message to the audience. There's no chance for interaction. Social Media is different. Social media allows you to be just that - *social!* Might as well take advantage of it and have a two-way conversation, right?

In the majority of your Live broadcasts, no matter

what your agenda is, you'll want to redirect their

attention to do something during or after your Live

show. But you have to ask for it. If you spend

100% of your time just broadcasting and 0% of

your time asking them to take action or make a

purchase, you'll get nowhere fast! In your overall

strategy for going Live on social media, you'll have

a combination of sales-y and non-sales-y

broadcasts, but let's talk about getting to the money

part first. It's all about the Benjamins, baby!

In business, you must ask for the sale. Rarely will

new people who find you be soooo excited about

making a purchase with you right there in the

moment that they'll need no guidance on how to actually make that transaction happen. Especially if it's their first time joining your Live show where you're trying to sell your products or services. Most people need you to spell it out for them and to make it as simple as possible. Eventually this book will be outdated and everyone will be not only knowledgeable about buying things through social media channels, but they'll be comfortable with it. We're not there yet, so expect some learning curve with your newbies who haven't experienced shopping with you before.

For instance, you can sell products during a Live broadcast on your Facebook business Page or Instagram profile. Let's say you're showing products you have in your on-hand inventory and

your audience members are able to claim what you

have by commenting on your video in real-time.

Then what? You can't magically reach through the

screen, collect their cash and in exchange give them

their products right then and there. I wish! Even

QVC and HSN make you wait for them to ship you

the products you just purchased. Nope, you must

tell them to *do* something next to kick off this

process of them getting their hands on your goodies

- and you getting paid..

How do you re-direct their attention?

Whether you're trying to sell them something or

not, here are some possible scenarios of what you

can ask them to do:

- Have them "Like" and "Share" your video

- Have them comment in real-time to be the
  first to claim something you're showing

- Have them fill out their contact information
  and shipping address through a form online

- Have them handle their invoices by
  checking their email after the show is over

You can also help "trick" the algorithm with a call
to action and have them comment certain things -
especially at the beginning of the Live broadcast.

Do you recall the part in Chapter 1 about the
Facebook algorithm? Well part of this next strategy

has to do with the algorithm.  On Facebook, for example, you're currently able to get up to 6x more engagement than any other type of post.

Engagement means likes, comments, shares...people joining and becoming an active part of your show. The quicker more people join and start taking action the more Facebook says, "Hey! This is good stuff....people are really liking this. Let's show it to more people in the Newsfeed..." New people join, they share to their networks and and soon you have more viewers joining.

To help encourage your Live audience to chime in and stop just passively watching you, ask them open-ended questions that require them to post an easy comment.  A comment is worth more than just

a person viewing you.

Some people who are going Live play games and

offer prizes or giveaways by having everyone make

a comment and then selecting a lucky random

winner.  This accomplishes both goals of 1) letting

Facebook's algorithm know that they've got a hot

Live show on their hands with lots of engaged

viewers and 2) that you're building rapport and

relationship and *value* with your audience.

Win-win! Think of ways to redirect them from just

simply watching to giving them an action to take

and see what happens.  Pro-tip: This can happen

throughout the broadcast, not just the beginning! If

you have a lull or start to see numbers of people

dropping, give the rest incentive to stay by playing a

quick game.  Even without giving a prize away,

playing trivia or just asking questions keeps people

entertained and interested.  Stay creative and

engaged with your audience and they'll hang with

you longer.


When I was selling jewelry on a Facebook Live, I

would try to give it a theme each time to stand out

from the others who were selling it, too.  For

example, one time I was packing up all of my things

to move to a new city for a few months to work on a

project.  I needed to sell as much inventory as I

could to lighten my load of things to pack.  The

theme I gave all three of my Live broadcasts that

week was about my move from Los Angeles.  As I

was showing pieces of jewelry for sale, I played

"Hollywood Trivia w/ Kerianne" and had them take

guesses in the comments for questions like, "Who

was the first celebrity I saw when I moved to Los

Angeles 11 years ago?" (Arnold Schwarzenegger,

the current Governor at the time). I also asked

things like, "Where is my son's favorite Los

Angeles landmark that has to do with stars?" Or,

"Who's my celebrity crush and Hollywood

husband?" (Jamie Foxx, who I'd met several times

and shared about on Facebook in the past). Those

who were my long-time friends who were shopping

and chatting with me on the Facebook Live were

quick to answer! It was fun and then I'd turn it

around and ask everyone watching: "So, who's *your*

celebrity crush?" The answers were super fun and

we all had a good time getting to know each other better (and all while I was selling jewelry and feeling so grateful to be able to reach through the lens and pick up money on the table.)

Since it's no longer the 90s and your audience isn't sitting around a TV screen watching a sitcom, they're able to sit around *your* screen and have legit, real conversations with you. Redirect them from just being a passive "watching" audience, to a more engaged audience by taking action during your Live broadcast. Take a minute to think about ways you can get creative and interactive with your audience and you'll have a fanbase who can't wait for you to go Live before you know it!

# Chapter Nine: Tips & Tricks

# for Going Live

### BEFORE You Go Live

All of these things should be done before you press

the button to go Live:

- Fix your hair

- Adjust your clothes

- Adjust your camera positioning

Do not waste the viewers time making them watch

you get yourself together.  Their attention span is

super small - don't give them a reason to leave!

Let the dog out. Have the kids situated in the other room. Adjust your lights. Clear the background mess. Put your phone on silent, vibrate or Airplane Mode. Do all the little things *before* you go Live.

## Introduction

Don't forget to introduce yourself every single time. It only takes one person who's new to stumble across your video and feel clueless of what's happening here. Make it clear right away.

And thank them for watching!

## Filters

Facebook and Instagram have a ton of funny, creative, interesting and sometimes even, weird, face filters. Try not to use these in such a way that it distracts the audience from your goal of your broadcast. It's ok to have a little fun, but looking like a small, baby wooded animal with fur might not be in the best interest of your brand. Use sparingly.

Use customized Live filters to give your broadcast an entirely unique look. Take advantage of branding yourself on screen when your audience is watching. This is a clever way to set yourself apart from the competition, too.

**<u>Be mindful of the #encore viewers.</u>**

Avoid delays during the first :30 seconds or so of
your Live broadcast.

Don't start a broadcast and make everyone wait
while you add people or invite several to share.
Have another person help you with this task, or wait
until you're in the flow of things to invite. Your
audience's attention is the most precious thing they
can give you so don't take it for granted by wasting
their time.

## Call them by name

Did you know the best sounding word to any one person is the sound of their name? It's the most important word they can hear. When someone joins your broadcast or leaves a comment or question, acknowledge them by name. By just adding this one simple strategy as often as you can, you'll make the audience feel more special and have them coming back for more.

## Portrait vs Landscape

Over 98% of Facebook is being viewed on a mobile device. This means when you're live, most people are watching you in the palm of their hands. Their phone is typically resting in a portrait (or tall way) version of their screen (not landscape, that's long and horizontal). Therefore, go Live where *you* are in portrait mode. This way you take up the whole screen and you appear closer to them. Also, when you flip your phone and go Live in landscape mode, the current layout for Facebook is only going to show you in the top ⅓ or so of the screen. The rest is white space for everyone's comments. I'd rather have you fill up the screen so we can see you (and the amazing products you may be trying to sell)! This is different, of course, when you have a guest or need more room for the both of you, but try to go Live in portrait mode.

## Ask Them to "Like" and "Share" Your Video

Be careful with this one...you're asking them to help YOU out, so don't take it for granted or get too comfortable saying it robotically.  Unless there's something in it for them, this might be hard to make happen.  People are more apt to help you out and share your video when they have a good relationship with you, but people are always going to take action when they're incentivized.

Enter the people who share your video into a contest and give away prizes for those who share.

Be sure to THANK EVERYONE.

## **Pinned Comments/Links:**

If you have an important thought or link to share during your broadcast, "pin" it at the top. By holding down the comment, you're able to keep that comment you made on the screen at all times. People can click through any hyperlink that's added to that comment, making it super easy for you to have them take whichever action you want.

## **Instant Weight Loss on Camera Tricks**

Angles are everything. If your camera is stationary during your broadcast, make sure your camera lens (that teeny, tiny camera lens on your phone) is directly across at your eye level. Looking directly into it (or even slightly UP at the camera lens) will make you appear the thinnest. Any angle where your camera lens is placed down below your eye level, you'll appear bigger. Not flattering! For a bonus tip, place your camera slightly above your eye contact line and tilt it down a bit.

## The Ceiling Isn't For Sale

Make sure your frame is set up correctly (refer to Chapter Five). Unless you're selling houses and ceilings are on sale, you'll want to make sure your camera doesn't showcase any part you don't want visible. You have a limited screen to work with anyhow. Use every inch wisely! Bring your camera down a bit. Position the camera so your head is near the top of the screen's frame.  Speaking of

ceilings, don't show a ceiling fan during your show.

It's quite dizzying and a visual distraction to

viewers.  I once left a jewelry show because I was

getting a headache! Be mindful of the viewer's

experience.


## Don't Hide Behind the Comments


Allow space for comments to live on the bottom

50% of your phone's screen.  If you're showing

products, make sure you either hold the products

*above* the comments (show them in the top half of

the screen).  When you're getting set up to go Live,

imagine the comments flowing in.  Make

adjustments to allow your viewers to shop easily

and without distractions and your sales will increase

## **Get the Ball Rolling with a Quick Sale**

One of my clients told me that she'll go Live to sell

jewelry and no one will make a move for awhile,

but as soon as one person claims a piece then they

all start buying after that.  Part of this is psychology.

And peer pressure.  Since everyone is shopping

together (and most likely amongst strangers) it may

feel awkward for them to claim things in front of

others.  But once the first person leads the way, it's

like a sign for everyone else that it's ok to do it, too.

Try your best to get that first purchase in the bag

asap. Jump start the momentum and keep the party

going!

## Windows: Friend or Foe?

During the daytime, windows shouldn't be

anywhere in your frame unless you have sufficient

light to counterbalance the blaring white light

coming through the glass. Move your camera a bit

more so it's out of the picture. A bright white light

from a window distracts people from watching you

on your stage. Better yet - *face* a window and use

all that glorious light. #getlit

**<u>Watch Your Words</u>**

Yes, I'm talking about best representing yourself
and the company with whom you've chosen to
partner. That's common sense. However, I'm also
talking about any visible words your viewer may
see on their screen - banners, slogans, websites,
words on your t-shirt, etc. The default setting on
Facebook's camera, for example, is going to show
everything BACKWARDS. Since most people
aren't proficient in reading backwards and you want
to best represent yourself and your company, either
remove the words or flip around your camera. Each
phone is different so look for your Settings on your
camera, or look for the magic wand on Facebook to
flip it the right way.

# Conclusion

It's your time to shine, my friend. Are you feeling ready to fully step into your digital spotlight?! I'm so proud of you for taking the time to invest in your biz and educate yourself on how to win in business today. Creating a solid social media presence is key to your success. Learning how to go Live to reach through the lens and pick up money on the table will help crush your overall strategy to build and grow your business. If you take what you've learned in this book, apply the strategies effectively and consistently, you're going to get to your goals much more quickly.

Be sure to connect with me online for further

coaching and support in my free Facebook group,

Kerianne's Money Makers.  Come find me here to

join:

www.facebook.com/groups/keriannesmoneymakers

.


I'll see you online, superstar.  Go be great!

Made in the USA
Columbia, SC
24 February 2019